GL 2.2 AR .5

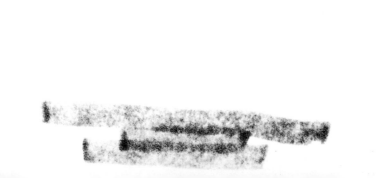

RIHANNA

RIGHT ON!

Gareth Stevens
Publishing

By Ella Rose

Please visit our website, www.garethstevens.com. For a free color catalog of all our high-quality books, call toll free 1-800-542-2595 or fax 1-877-542-2596.

Library of Congress Cataloging-in-Publication Data

Rose, Ella.
Rihanna / Ella Rose.
    p. cm. — (Hip-hop headliners)
Includes index.
ISBN 978-1-4339-6618-7 (pbk.)
ISBN 978-1-4339-6619-4 (6-pack)
ISBN 978-1-4339-6616-3 (library binding)
1. Rihanna, 1988—Juvenile literature. 2. Singers—Biography—Juvenile literature. I. Title.
ML3930.R55R67 2012
782.42164092—dc23
[B]

                              2011031096

First Edition

Published in 2012 by
Gareth Stevens Publishing
111 East 14th Street, Suite 349
New York, NY 10003

Copyright © 2012 Gareth Stevens Publishing

Designer: Haley W. Harasymiw
Editor: Therese M. Shea

Photo credits: Cover background Shutterstock.com; cover, p. 1 (Rihanna) Dan MacMedan/ Getty Images; p. 5 Ethan Miller/Getty Images; p. 7 Bryan Bedder/Getty Images; pp. 9, 27 Kevin Winter/Getty Images; p. 11 Frazer Harrison/Getty Images; p. 13 New York Daily News Archive/Getty Images; p. 15 Evan Agostini/Getty Images; p. 17 Rajesh Jantilal/Getty Images; p. 19 Stringer/Getty Images; p. 21 Kevin Mazur/WireImage/Getty Images; p. 23 Lucy Nicholson/AFP/Getty Images; p. 25 Steve Jennings/WireImage/Getty Images; p. 29 Mike Coppola/Getty Images.

Printed in the United States of America

CPSIA compliance information: Batch #CW12GS: For further information contact Gareth Stevens, New York, New York at 1-800-542-2595.

Contents

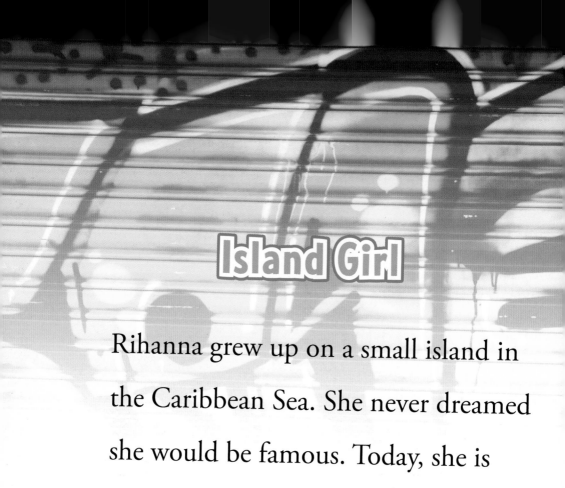

Island Girl

Rihanna grew up on a small island in the Caribbean Sea. She never dreamed she would be famous. Today, she is one of the biggest stars in music.

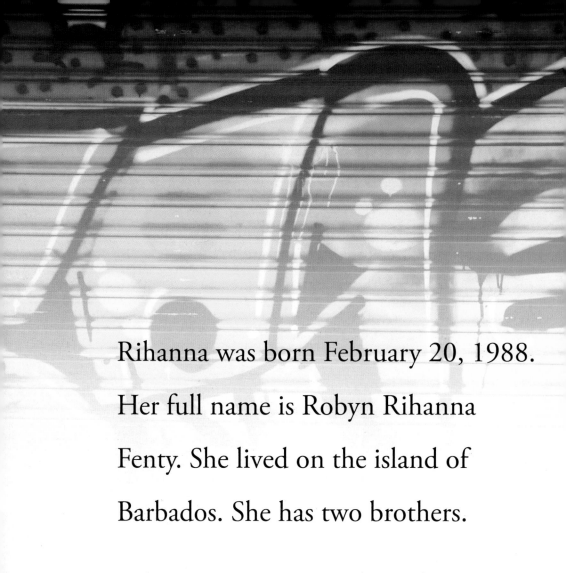

Rihanna was born February 20, 1988.
Her full name is Robyn Rihanna
Fenty. She lived on the island of
Barbados. She has two brothers.

Shy Singer

When Rihanna was young, her parents often fought. This made Rihanna sad and shy. Singing made her happy. She and two friends formed a music group.

Many people like to take trips to Barbados. One of these people was a music producer from New York City. He first heard Rihanna sing in 2003. He knew she could be a star.

In 2004, the producer asked Rihanna to fly to New York City. There, she sang for Jay-Z. He was the president of Def Jam Records. He wanted her to make an album.

Jay-Z

Albums and Hits

In 2005, Rihanna put out her first album. It was called *Music of the Sun*. She mixed music from her island home into her songs. Rihanna went on tour with Gwen Stefani.

15

In 2006, Rihanna's second album came out. It was called *A Girl Like Me*. It had two number 1 songs on it. One was called "S.O.S."

Rihanna's third album was named *Good Girl Gone Bad*. The song "Umbrella" was on the music charts for months. She won a Grammy for it, too!

In 2009, *Rated R* came out. "Rude Boy" was another number 1 hit for Rihanna. She also sang a song with Jay-Z and Kanye West. It was called "Run This Town."

Kanye West

Jay-Z

Rihanna's album *Loud* came out in 2010. Her song with hip-hop star Drake hit number 1 on the charts. It was called "What's My Name?"

Drake

Giving Back

In 2006, Rihanna started a group called Believe. It helps children in need. She works with other children's groups, too.

Style

Rihanna is known for her special style. She likes to change her hair color. She dresses to be different. This star turns heads wherever she goes.

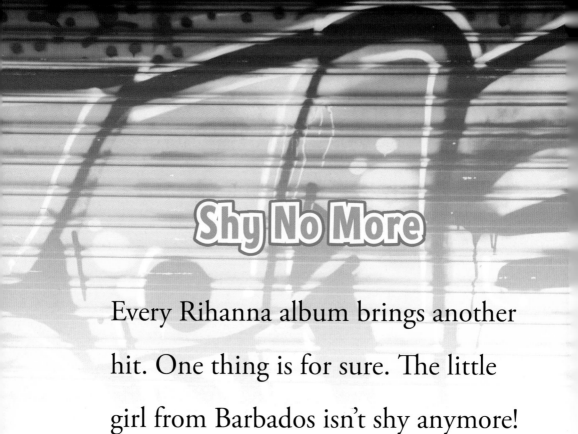

Shy No More

Every Rihanna album brings another hit. One thing is for sure. The little girl from Barbados isn't shy anymore!

Timeline

1988   Rihanna is born February 20 on Barbados.

2003   Rihanna sings for a music producer.

2004   Rihanna sings for Jay-Z at Def Jam Records.

2005   Rihanna's first album comes out.

2006   "S.O.S" becomes a number 1 song.

2008   Rihanna wins a Grammy for "Umbrella."

2010   Rihanna's album *Loud* tops the hip-hop music chart.

For More Information

Books

Edwards, Laurie J. *Rihanna*. Detroit, MI: Lucent Books, 2009.

Heos, Bridget. *Rihanna*. New York, NY: Rosen Publishing Group, 2011.

Krumenauer, Heidi. *Rihanna*. Hockessin, DE: Mitchell Lane Publishing, 2009.

Websites

Rihanna

www.islanddefjam.com/artist/home.aspx?artistID=7366
Read the latest news about Rihanna.

Rihanna

www.billboard.com/artist/rihanna/658897#/artist/rihanna/658897
Read more about Rihanna's life and see how her music is doing on the charts.

Glossary

Grammy: an honor given to someone for their music

producer: one who helps make a piece of music

record: a copy of music that can be played again and again

style: a special look

tour: a trip to many places in order to play and sing music for people

Index